AF583799

for
Barbara
and
Sonja

Chris McKimmie

FORD ST

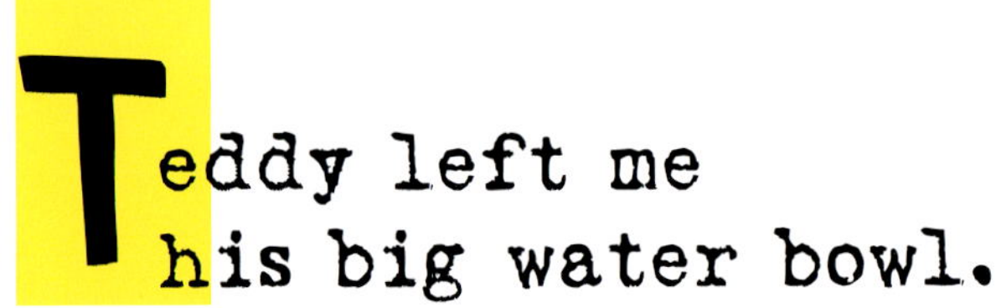

Teddy left me
his big water bowl.

His food bowl.

Two couches
to sleep on.

Two nice and snuggly
futon beds
and also
a king size bed
I share
with the humans.

I have a box full of other
stuff too.

Le Woof

Maisie bought me
seven stuffed lobsters.
I have two left.
I chewed the rest up.
I love chewing
things.

I have two dolls,
one duck, a tea pot
and a pot plant
to play with.
And a Leo the Lion.

With my tea pot and orange blanky I can pretend

to
be
an
elephant.

Shirl!
It's another
Mr. Scary!
Roll it round on the
ROLL ROLL ROLL ROLL ROLL ROLL ROLL

I
can
chuck
my
pot
plant
up
in
the
blue
sky.

Roll
it
round
on
the
ground.

ROLL ROLL ROLL ROLL ROLL ROLL ROLL ROLL ROLL

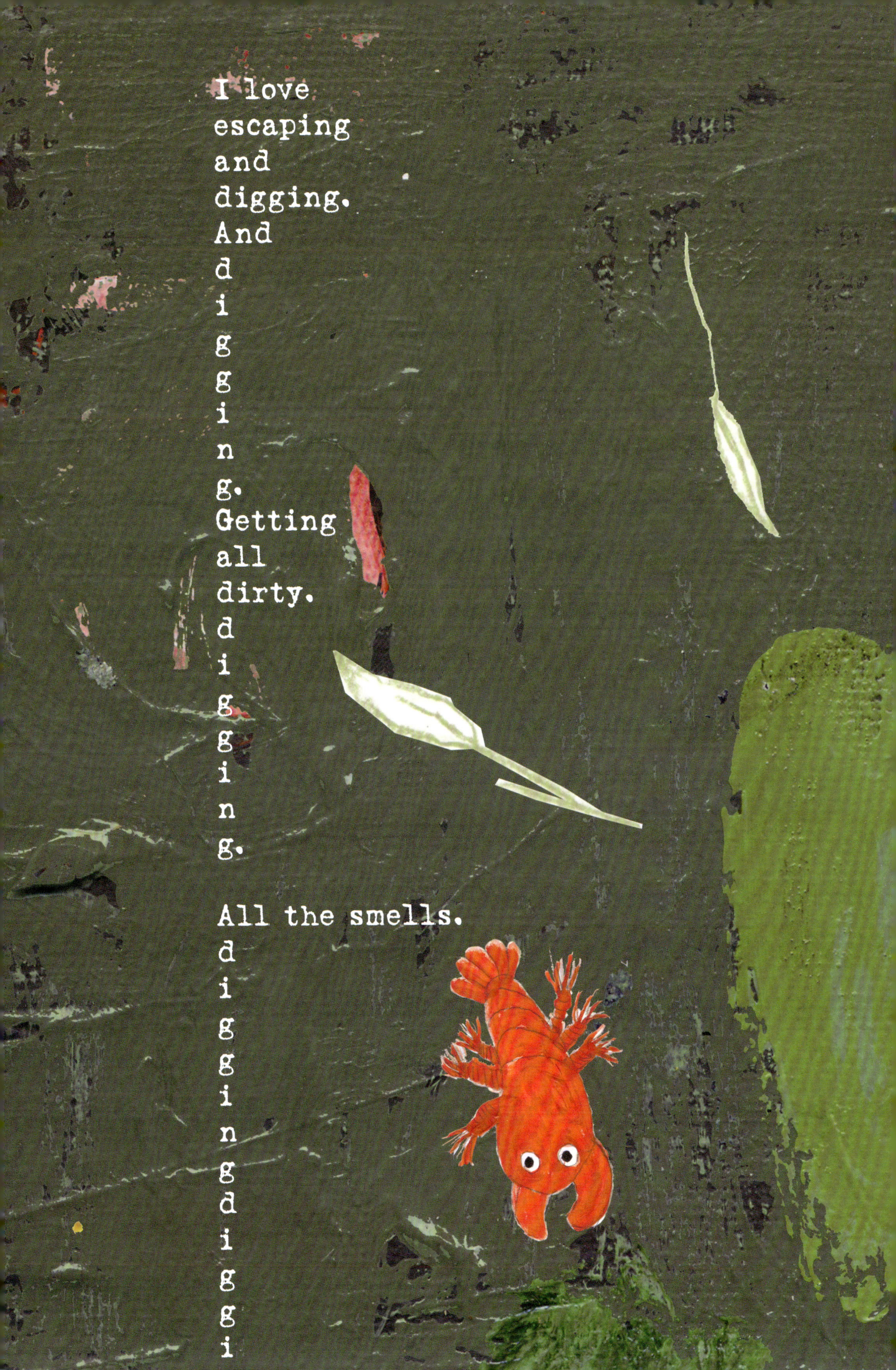

I love
escaping
and
digging.
And
d
i
g
g
i
n
g.
Getting
all
dirty.
d
i
g
g
i
n
g.

All the smells.
d
i
g
g
i
n
g
d
i
g
g
i

Don't
like
bath
times.

RUMBLE
R U M B L E

Scared of storms.

I am
very
very
clever.

junior
GOODNESS
Champion
BEST AT
SIT STAY
LIE DOWN
LEAVE IT
ROLL OVER
WAIT
Kiddo.

Marcus made a painting of me.
I was a model for him
in his art class.
I am a
model
dog.

PETE'S No.
POTATOES

I
like the
kitchen.
One day
I ate a
whole
loaf of
bread in
a plastic
bag.

It
made
me sick
all
the next
day.

All
day.

I love
books.

I love eating
cushions
and
paper too.

All sorts
of stuff really.

I love
barking at
birds.

Barking at
possums at night,
too.

Sometimes
just barking.

KIDDO!
COME INSIDE!

I love
the
patche

of
warm
s u n s h i n e
in my
yard.

I am

Kiddo.

The new dog.

Notes for Vets,

Saturday

Kiddo drank salt water at Nudgee beach.

Ate compost at Blake and Barbara's place.

Sunday Morning

Really crook

Listless

Dazed

Confused

Had to be carried into house

Monday morning

Back to normal

Monday night

ate 9 packets of potatoechips* from pantry.

* the small ones.

I should change his name to garbage guts

Teddy ate ~~[illegible]~~ anything

But Kiddo leaves him for dead!

© Words images design
Chris McKimmie 2022

First published by
Ford Street Publishing
Melbourne, Victoria
Australia
2 4 6 8 10 9 7 5 3 1
This publication is copyright.
Apart from any use as permitted under the Copyright Act 1968, no part may be reproduced by any process without prior written permission from the publisher.

Requests and enquiries concerning reproduction should be addressed to
Ford Street Publishing Pty Ltd
162 Hoddle Street
Abbotsford
Vic 3067
Australia

The painting of Kiddo is by Marcus McKimmie

The head of the orange doll is by Maisie McKimmie

Hardback ISBN 9781922696038
Paperback ISBN 9781922696045

A catalogue record for this book is available from the National Library of Australia

Printed in China by Tingleman Pty Ltd